Meanderings

Betty McKenzie-Tubb

Meanderings

Acknowledgements

I'd like to thank the family members and all those lovely writing friends who have lent me their ears and given me encouragement.

In particular, I'd like to express my gratitude to Robyn Mathison, who suggested I join FAW (Fellowship of Australian Writers) Tasmania. Thus I was introduced to Jen Gibson and Shirley Burke, without whose sacrificial and practical help (each engaged in their own serious writing) these words would never have seen the light of day.

Meanderings
ISBN 978 1 76041 215 9
Copyright © text Betty McKenzie-Tubb 2016
Cover design: Allana Blizzard Jones

First published 2016 by
GINNINDERRA PRESS
PO Box 3461 Port Adelaide 5015
www.ginninderrapress.com.au

Contents

A Passion for Pencils	7
A Diet of Worms	9
A Letter of Excuse, 2 April 1580	12
An Unexpected Wedding	14
'Chief Nourisher'	16
Face	18
Feet-blind Reverence	21
Hoist With My Own Petard	23
In Praise of the Full Sentence	27
Look at Me! Look at ME!	30
My Room 101	33
Not Eden	35
Red	37
The Fix	40
Terrorists on the Café Strip	43
The Lowbrow: a response to her critics…	45
The Men in my Life	48
'To Be or Not to Be'	50
What's in a Name?	52
Gone but not Forgotten – a Eulogy	54
'There's a Divinity that Shapes our Ends'	58
Surviving without Fractions and Dots	61
Luxury	64
The Evocation of Colour	66
Lexical Gold	68
Legs – a female view	70

Bogans	72
Uncle	74
The Winner Is…	77

A Passion for Pencils

Virginia Woolf may have thought that nobody could feel passionately towards a lead pencil but then she'd never met Dawn French – or me, for that matter.

Her essay *Street Haunting* opens with the sentence, 'No one perhaps has ever felt passionately towards a lead pencil', but, in the manner of personal essays, she temporarily leaves the subject of lead pencils and sticks more closely to her subtitle, 'A London adventure', in which she describes the magic of walking London streets on a winter night. (Woolf died in 1941, so that magic may no longer exist.)

Only at the conclusion of the essay does she return to the trigger of her musings, the peg on which she hangs her thoughts; then the reader may be convinced of her affection for the instrument.

> And here – let us examine it tenderly, touch it with reverence – is the only spoil we have retrieved from all the treasures of the city, a lead pencil.

There are writers who, like Tim Winton and the late Elizabeth Jolley, eschew the computer and use pen on paper. The remarkable and truly talented P.D. James at the age of ninety wrote her latest novel by hand, and at ninety-two was producing yet another opus in the same manner. She may use a pen but I like to think that she favours the speed of the pencil.

Dawn French has written her two novels with a pencil. She confesses to being a Luddite, though I doubt whether she rages around smashing every computer in sight. She enjoys the smell of the pencil, the sound it makes when put to the paper. She thinks that writing in this mode is 'more organic'.

The sight of two or three newly sharpened pencils is a pretty one.

They beg to be taken up and used. Of course, the tool has to be the right one or it won't slide easily over the paper. A 2B, once commonly used by schoolchildren, is excellent. It makes a brave mark and glides smoothly. Idly leafing through some books recently, I read that the dying Venerable Bede directed someone at his bedside to 'Take your pen, put it in order, and write quickly.' That's exactly what a newly sharpened 2B does and it's a lovely sensation.

Some people are in love with pens and there are those who despise the admittedly useful biro in favour of the fountain pen. My history with pens is not a good one. In the pen and ink schooldays when one was fooled into thinking that being an ink monitor was a privilege, or even a reward for being good, my nibs invariably crossed and caused a fine splatter of ink which a modern abstract artist could claim as some kind of conceptual work – the randomness of the universe, perhaps – but which my teachers regarded with disapproval and deemed it to be what it was – a mess. My fingers too were constantly ink-stained and I developed a callus on my middle finger where the pen, held correctly between thumb and forefinger, nevertheless rested on the middle one. Even biros seem to develop little blobs of ink on the tips and these deposit themselves on the fingers or worse, on the paper.

No, the pencil is king. It is cheap, it uses some form of solar energy (that of the body, some sage asserted). When errors occur, they are simply erased; it is easily maintained and if it 'crashes' there's a sharpener on hand. If great writers of yore managed to produce enduring masterpieces without the so-called advantage of technology, do we really think, as some would have us believe, that we write better when we use a computer?

I'm off to write a few deathless lines with my 2B.

A Diet of Worms

Who amongst us has not been on a diet of some kind? Diets for specific illnesses, for allergies, for optimum health, for the perfect figure.

The perfect figure is probably the most common and the most elusive. Appalled by the present epidemic of obesity, we've become obsessed with slimness, desiring (and I suppose this applies particularly to women) a stick figure. This is extremely difficult for those of us who have inherited fat-trapping genes. I belong to this group but when some of my overweight friends discipline themselves and lose tens of kilos, I feel quite sad because I'd rather have more of them than less, and anyway their faces cease to be plump and smiling and become lined and doleful. Face or figure: that's the choice.

In the search for a svelte shape, we try, among others, the Israel diet, the Atkin diet, Jenny Craig, Weight Watchers, the current Paleo diet. As I recall, there was a chocolate diet which must have had universal if temporary appeal, though I am not sure that it worked – perhaps it comprised a Mars bar reward after a plate of lettuce.

In history, when I was a schoolgirl, my attention was once torn from the 'poetry' (only readers will be aware of the inverted commas around that word) I was writing under my desk, by the teacher's mention of a diet of worms. I was both baffled and revolted but imagined it must have been some kind of European remedy for the plague. I believe I was called upon to write something about it in a later history exam and, not having engaged in any research pertaining to the diet, I did not score a very high mark. I almost certainly wrote utter rubbish akin to what I penned about an equally mysterious subject, the Rotten Boroughs. Surprisingly they had nothing to do with village composting.

Anyway, it was much later – too late to earn me an exalted grade – that

I learned that Diet is a meeting and Worms – or V3ms as depicted by the international phonetic alphabet – is a town in West Germany where, in 1521, Martin Luther was outlawed by the emperor Charles V. His great crime was to cry out against the sale of indulgences, which were not goodies like chocolate or champagne but, roughly speaking, tickets to heaven. But no doubt you know all that.

How interesting but how confusing is history for young people grappling with diets of worms, rotten boroughs, tennis court oaths and the like. Were the next diet one of worms, I am sure it would be most effective in reducing weight, assuming that the candidates, sick with revulsion, had not already died of starvation.

There's a book titled, I think, *Why French Women Don't Get Fat*. It apparently points out that treats like cheese, cream, butter and wine are not omitted from the French cuisine. The reason French females do not get fat (what – never?) is because they eat such things as small portions. Have you noticed the latest tendency in Australian restaurants is to present overladen plates of food? Alas, some of us eat the lot, *because we pay for it*.

Of course if you dine at really expensive establishments where you pay astronomical prices for minuscule quantities served on huge white plates decorated with what appear to be drops of blood ('plating', I believe it is called) you may well lose weight, unless you hurry home and consume piles of hot buttered toast to fill the yawning hole which is your stomach.

The golden rule is moderation in all things but let me tell you, in words not my own, the real cause of morbid obesity. Don't stop me, even if you have heard it before:

1 Japanese eat very little fat and suffer fewer heart attacks than *British, Americans or Australians*.
2 Mexicans eat lots of fat and suffer fewer heart attacks than *British, Americans or Australians*.
3 Chinese drink very little red wine and suffer fewer heart attacks than *British, Americans or Australians*.
4 Italians drinks excessive amounts of red wine and also suffer fewer heart attacks than *British, Americans or Australians*.

5 Germans drink a lot of beer, eat lots of sausages and fats and suffer fewer heart attacks than *British, Americans or Australians*.

Conclusion: eat and drink whatever you like! Speaking English is apparently what kills you.

A Letter of Excuse, 2 April 1580

Dear Juliet,

The night we spent together, though threatened by your pesky nurse, was bliss, without a doubt. We both thought it was a prelude to our marriage, but I have had time to think very seriously about this proposed action and, to be blunt and no doubt cruel, I have to tell you that I have changed my mind.

Before I met you, I was in love with Rosaline, unfortunately also a Capulet, but the Capulet women do seem to be greatly superior to the Montagues, in beauty and intellect.

To return to the point: I was and still am, my heart tells me, in love with Rosaline and plan to try once more to woo and win her. She is the one I wish to have as a wife. I cannot believe that she really wishes to remain chaste and I am sure that I can change her mind.

Please do not carry out the plan to meet me at Friar Laurence's. I shall send my servant to him at once to tell him that our marriage will not take place. He was very surprised that I had so quickly transferred my affections from Rosaline to you, so will accept the situation with resignation.

Juliet, I know you have a passionate nature and are prone, I think, to impulsive and perhaps dangerous actions, so please keep that little jewelled dagger, a strange gift from some deranged Capulet, well away from your person. Try to be calm and rational about this change of plan.

It would be wise for you to look kindly upon that decent young man, Count Paris, who is rich, gallant and handsome. What is more, he is greatly favoured by your parents. He is seriously earnest in his desire to wed you and is obviously more reliable than I.

Thank you for the brief but wonderful time we spent together but pray keep away from that snooping Will Shakespeare. He'd make a sensational story out of anything and we do not want that, do we?

With very best wishes for the future,
Yours very sincerely,
    Romeo Montague.

An Unexpected Wedding

As people of mature age, most of us have attended many weddings in our lifetimes, some of them hugely formal and expensive, others informal and sometimes downright quirky.

No doubt, we women have all been bridesmaids, occasionally groaning at having to wear the dresses chosen by the bride – what looks good on a six-foot brunette does not necessarily become a five-foot blonde.

When I taught at a school managed by a board and not the Education Department, I was able to seek employment in the school holidays. This I often did in order to earn extra money for travel or some other indulgence. During one Christmas vacation, I worked behind the counter at Coles in Sydney, a store unlike Cole's supermarket. Pegs and other domestic aids were on sale. The permanent shop assistant in charge of the counter was a very pleasant woman who was probably in her thirties, though then I considered her to be quite old. Her name was Thelma and we got on famously together. One day, to my surprise, she told me that she was soon to be married and that she would like me to be her bridesmaid if I would consent to the proposal. There was really no reason not to agree, so I did. She then invited me to visit her home and to meet her fiancé.

I have to confess with some shame that when we had decided on a date and time and she gave me her address, I was disconcerted to learn that she lived in Redfern, which at that time was not, to put it mildly, a desirable location. I found it difficult to imagine her in such a setting.

The day of the visit arrived. My new friend's house was typical of that area but very clean and tidy. Her fiancé was an agreeable man, a Greek, somewhat older than she.

We discussed the wedding and what I should wear. Predictably enough, the colour was to be pink, made in whatever style I liked. The best man, my partner, would be a young Greek friend of theirs. Perhaps he was a relation, I really do not know; nor can I recall his name or that of the groom. My clever dress-making aunt used all her imagination and skill to make a suitable garment for me. *Then* I was pleased with it, though in retrospect I think I looked a bit like the fat fairy in *Iolanthe*. The skirt was of net over some shiny material – taffeta, maybe – and the hem was scalloped and piped with silver. Quite a sturdy girl, I looked no better when I was bridesmaid yet again, dressed this time in blue and with a big hat tied under the chin. I looked rather like a dim shepherdess.

My memory of the wedding and reception is hazy except that I am sure a good time was had by all. My aunt and uncle had been invited to the wedding and did attend but left early, having made sure that the best man would take me home when the celebrations ended. Rather trusting of them really, though the trust was not misplaced. The young man was perfectly well behaved and the brief kiss we shared was a 'goodnight' and 'goodbye' one. We never saw each other again.

The school holiday ended. I visited Thelma only once after the marriage. Our future paths never crossed but it was a strange and pleasant interlude in my life and I hope that those two nice people, my transitory friend and her Greek husband, lived happily ever after.

'Chief Nourisher'

Shakespeare always gets it right.

On some nights I, like many others, I've no doubt, toss and turn in bed and cannot sleep. I think about the members of my family, about their futures which I will not see; about my friends who are dead and how I wish I had said this or that to them; about more mundane things, like what I should add to my grocery shopping list and what I should have for dinner on the morrow. I write (in my head) reams of essays and lines of poetry which end nowhere.

So I understand Macbeth when he mourns his inability to sleep, longing for

> Sleep that knits up the ravelled sleave of care,
> the death of each day's life, sore labour's bath,
> balm of hurt minds, great nature's second course,
> chief nourisher in life's feast. (*Macbeth*, Act 2, Scene 2)

I try the recommendations for sleep inducement: emptying the mind; counting sheep; counting backwards from one hundred; concentrating on breathing in, holding to the count of three, out; hot milk; eating some carbohydrate (useless, but my favourite).

My dear husband used to advise, 'Just close your eyes and go to sleep.' He was able to do it but I could not and cannot.

If I have been tossing and turning for hours, I sometimes disentangle myself from the bedclothes which make me look like an Egyptian mummy, totter to the kitchen and make myself a bowl of porridge. Fortunately I do not have to stir with a spurtle for an interminable time; three minutes in the microwave oven does the trick. My theory is that in eating this good old Scottish fare, energy will drain from my brain to my stomach and the process of digestion. Sometimes this seems to work but at other times it is just a comforting diversion.

Of course, even when sleep comes, it does not come unattended. There is a trap and didn't Shakespeare know it. There is always the possibility that 'wicked dreams abuse / the curtained sleep'. (*Macbeth*, Act 1, Scene 7)

Shakespeare's other tortured soul, Hamlet, also knew the dangers of sleep, even as he believed in an afterlife, in the final one: 'to sleep,' he says, 'perchance to dream; aye there's the rub; For in that sleep…what dreams may come…' (*Hamlet*, Act 3, Scene 1)

On this day, Remembrance Day, I listened to some of the poems of Siegfried Sassoon and Wilfred Owen, who well knew the awfulness of dreams. Their experiences of war are replicated over and over again and there are many young men similarly haunted and who, unlike me, dread sleep.

There are other less serious reasons for troubled sleep or lack of it. What young parents have not suffered? When I was a sleep-deprived young mother, I remember adorning the door of my fridge with a paper bearing the words –

> No high ambition do I crave,
> Before my eyes I keep this aim;
> Just once before I die
> To get sufficient sleep.

Well, it does happen now for much of the time, though I penned these lines at two a.m. Even as I write, the porridge which I recently consumed seems to be working its magic. Now that I have written this little piece, I can think of no better words with which to close than those of the Bard (*Antony & Cleopatra*, Act 4, Scene 8): '…the task's done / and we must sleep.' He always gets it right.

Face

I dream a lot and my dreams are seldom pleasant, just falling short of nightmares, though I have those too. For this reason, I choose to select something cheerful or even comical for my bedtime reading.

Last night, I decided to trawl through a book of comic verse that was given to me recently. All of its own account, it opened at a verse by Sir Walter Raleigh. You may know it. It goes,

> I wish I loved the human race;
> I wish I loved its silly face;
> I wish I loved the way it walks;
> I wish I loved the way it talks;
> And when I'm introduced to one
> I wish I thought WHAT JOLLY FUN.

These words of disillusionment are not from the pen of the cloak-laying Sir Walter Raleigh of Elizabethan times but of his namesake who lived from 1861 to 1922. He was the first holder of the Chair of English Literature at Oxford. With some delight, I notice that each line, apart from the last two, end with a semicolon so – not to wander entirely from the subject of face – on the *face* of it, it would seem that this later Raleigh was quite in favour of that particular punctuation mark, now so unfashionable.

The verse is exactly in harmony with my feelings. More than ever, it seems, humankind is showing its ugly face. What makes us different from other animals is the knowledge of good and evil. We have a choice and that choice seems weighted towards the latter: prolonged detention of asylum seekers in unpleasant and even dangerous conditions; the disinclination of Australia to give sanctuary to people who are fleeing persecution; the plight of women in countries like Afghanistan, Saudi Arabia and Africa. The list goes on and, to a lesser degree, Australia is no exception.

We are all descendants of boat people; people who wished to lead a better life, to escape from poverty and sometimes from a disgraceful class system, the remnants of which remain. Many, of course were criminals, minor and major, but most redeemed themselves and contributed to the building of our society, once a source of pride.

But to the personal. Every morning – how can I word it? The face has to be faced. I speak for myself when I say that it is not the most pleasant introduction to the day.

'My face,' said the poet W.H. Auden, 'looks like a wedding cake left out in the rain.' And that describes mine exactly.

I do not want to frighten the natives, so I spend some time trying to reconstruct the cake. Cosmetics are not a great help. Too much only serves to highlight the cracks. However, application of a bit of bright lipstick takes away from the general greyness of the face. A comb of the hair and that is about as much as I can do.

'It's your character that counts,' said the voice of the elders, but that could do with a bit of spit and polish, too. 'Smile,' say the voices. A grandchild's question – 'Why are your teeth brown, Gran'ma?' – does not encourage me to give a toothy grin.

It is interesting that the face is sometimes called 'dial' and 'clock'. The latter is a most apt synonym because it certainly registers the passing of time and its legacy of ruin. Lauren Bacall, who had little to worry about, spoke nice words of comfort: 'I think your whole life shows on your face and you should be proud of that.'

Mind you, if your life has been misspent, that window may not be comforting. My own next meeting with my mirror may tell me something I don't want to know.

Last night I was trying to think of a suitable conclusion to this piece before you fall asleep through boredom. Nothing came except a sudden remembrance of an essay by Robert Benchley in *The Art of the Personal Essay – an Anthology from the Classical Era to the Present* (edited by Phillip

Lapote, 1994, Anchor Books). It is short and amusing and actually titled 'My Face'. I wish that his concluding words were mine. I am going to use them without his permission. He died in 1945 and I don't think he would mind:

> ...whatever is in store for me, I shall watch the daily modulations (of my face) with an impersonal fascination not unmixed with awe at Mother Nature's gift for caricature, and will take the bitter with the sweet and keep a stiff upper lip.

Feet-blind Reverence

If I were a fetishist, the object of my fascination might be feet. When I say this, I'm not of course referring to those which are corned, callused or distorted, but to those which are smallish, delicate and white with perfect toes capped with pink, translucent nails. Most of us will remember the sheer delight of cupping in our hands the tiny, perfect feet of babies, those not yet encased by shoes, the corollaries of feet and also a minor personal obsession.

On a recent visit to Melbourne, I was looking for shoes to wear to a coming family wedding and visited the new Collins Street store of Peter Sheppard, doyen of exquisite shoes. It's an Aladdin's cave of footwear, much of it glittering appropriately in the season of bling and, it must be said, unwearable by the generally damaged feet of the ageing. Bunions and ridged horny nails cannot be enhanced by over-priced jewelled thongs or sandals.

It's impossible not to mention the ubiquitous and usually grubby jogger, no longer an unwelcome stranger in any society. Perhaps they are cleaner and more expensive seen on the street in the more salubrious suburbs, and often the wearers really do jog, but they are also worn by the smart set to trendy restaurants, to the theatre, to the opera, as accompaniments to designer jeans. Has more hideous foot covering ever been devised?

If we are to be honest, we'll confess to assessing people by their clothes, at least initially and often wrongly, but whereas the observer's eye commonly travels from head to toe, mine travels from feet to head. So much can be revealed by a person's shoes. Earnest Greenies – and I don't speak of them in a derogatory way – tend to wear 'Blunnies', Homipeds, Kumfs or Birkenstocks (the latter prescribed for the patient of one GP as the perfect contraceptive). Non-aligned but sensible women with healthy self-esteem also wear commonsensical shoes, well cared for and even polished, contrasting with grubby falsely designated low care faux suede – Nubuck. The young sport the mandatory bling or sandals, thongs or ballet shoes; toes painted red, purple or even gothic black. Women intent on getting to the top in the corporate world or who are professionals lean towards pumps, usually black and shiny with moderately high heels.

Heels are an issue. Fortunately, the fashion-conscious capable of forward thinking are able to select attractive low-heeled footwear which is at the same time smart and pretty. Perhaps these sensible women have viewed with distaste the feet of those mothers and grandmothers who in their youth squeezed their feet into pointy-toed shoes with four-inch heels, not realising that they were tottering towards big toes set at right angles to the rest and the size of small eggs.

It's sad to see the return of arrowhead-toed shoes and heels sometimes five inches high. These are often relatively cheap because very poorly designed. I can't be the only one who considers them grotesque. I'm suddenly reminded of the cruel miniaturisation which resulted in the 'lily feet' of Chinese ladies and wonder that some women in our own culture quite voluntarily deform theirs.

Booted feet are another category. Thigh-high boots are sexy, perhaps only because they are worn by those with perfect legs. Men in boots are bushwalkers, farmers, labourers or, if they are in sinister shiny black, bikies. I have to confess to rather liking hearing Nancy Sinatra singing, 'These boots are made for walking / and that's just what they'll do / One of these days these boots are going / to walk all over you.' A nice little feminist ditty to sing to a very macho man.

One could write about feet as in measurement, as bases of objects, as metrical units in verse and so on, as well as in phrases like 'get off on the wrong foot', but the perfect anatomical foot is surely the most enticing subject for a slight written piece.

Hoist With My Own Petard

...as usual.

Who suggested to her peers that they write about the UPSIDE of growing old? In their 70s and 80s, as am I, there are always plenty of moans about ill-health, the loss of those dear to them, the diminishing acuity of the senses, the – well, the list is endless. Surely, I said, there must be some advantages in ageing?

So far there have been no written words on the subject forthcoming and I am not surprised. My scheme has backfired and I have been struggling for weeks to evoke the blessings of anility. The task is not easy but I am continuing to try.

I am in my eighty-seventh year. It is only recently that I have felt and concluded that I am old. People have suddenly become inordinately kind, offering to help me when actually I have not needed help. This kindness has reminded me (in a time when we need reminding, such is the awfulness of our present world) that most people *are* kind and good. I now admit, because it is true, that a helping hand as I descend from the bus, or climb staircases which have no handrail, is most welcome and I give the helper heartfelt thanks.

You can see, I hope, that I am pointing out one of the blessings of old age: the restoration of faith in humankind.

Living alone, as most women have to in the third age, does not seem at first to offer any benefits, especially when a person has not lived alone for a very long time – perhaps never, if there has been no period of independence between living in the parental home and transitioning to the marital one. However, there *are* joys in independence, not the least being that one can lie diagonally in the big bed and eat porridge in the wee small hours of the morning, if one is so disposed.

More seriously, there is the opportunity to pursue interests, even passions like the passion for writing. If the latter, you can hum a little ditty.

> Nothing now in the world I lack;
> I'm free to be a graphomaniac.

Meals can wait until one's opus is completed. That is, if one is not as greedy as I am – one who is always eager for a meal, but it can be had at any time. We do not have to be like poor Shirley Valentine before her emancipation. In the bad old days, many a little compliant housewife endangered her health and mental well-being by endeavouring to place the evening meal on the table at six o'clock (or whatever time was decreed by the master) *sharp*.

There is the joy of making decisions. They are not always the right ones but it is nice not to have to be accountable to anyone else for one's folly. And oh, the bliss of making the sound one. It does happen.

Probably the enormous plus of old age comes with the advent of grandchildren and, as in my own case, of great-grandchildren. It is interesting and such a privilege to watch them grow and mature and it is a cause for joy when and if they morph into responsible, caring adults. It is a source of pride when they are successful in their chosen careers. It is a great thing to be an observer, relieved not to have the responsibility of parenting.

But we are *grand*parents. We can be mentors. I have heard so many people acknowledging the good influence of their grandparents, most commonly grandmothers, it must be said, and commenting on the significance of their presence in their lives. I myself was moved to tears to receive a card from my youngest granddaughter which bore the message:

To my beautiful Grandma.
    Thank you for being such a wonderful friend and mentor. I appreciate you SO much.

In case you think that is an anecdote of self-praise, I assure you it is not. I do not consider myself beautiful in any sense but I am glad that she sees me that way and may the veil never be lifted from her eyes.

Grandchildren often declare that they have been influenced more by these old ones than by their own parents. Perhaps this is because grandparents usually have more time to talk and discuss. Importantly, time to listen. The benefit is mutual. We have so much to learn from the young.

There is another plus for old women. You may have noticed that I have used the old word 'anility' instead of the more usual 'senility'. I will tell you why, and it is a recent and joyous discovery. The word 'senile' comes from, and I quote, the 'French *senile* or Latin *senilus*, from *senex*, old man'. So you see, as a woman and liberal feminist, I rejoice that women cannot possibly be senile *ever*!

The University of the Third Age (U3A) is a gift to those inhabiting that time. No need for the brain to stagnate. The classes taken by the most able of tutors, often retired and distinguished academics but, if not, always at the top their particular tree, encompass many areas. Do you want to brush up your Shakespeare, read and write poetry, learn to paint, master a new language? The list is endless. I do not know who Charles Handy is or was but he wisely said, 'The Third Age is the opportunity to be someone different, if we want to be.'

Christmas has just passed. No longer was I the one preparing the feast or engaging in the cleaning of the often neglected spaces. I did not have to clear the dining table where there are books and papers for which there is no longer room on my study desk. I did not have to deck the halls with boughs of holly, though I did sing, 'Tra la la la la la la la la.' I was transported to my daughter's house for a champagne breakfast and afterwards was quite content to accept the role of the 'Aged P' in the corner, not minding at all to be acknowledged with a smile and random hugs from the members of three generations.

I am a bit Scroogie and abjure the big Christmas dinner, so was driven home. I then spent the rest of the day with like-minded friends, eating simply and tippling just a little.

I feel increasingly positive about the hitherto dreaded O.A. as I write. My daughter once said to me that if she feels down she tries to think of at least five blessings every day. Surprisingly, it is quite easy to think of more.

Spike Milligan had a great try when he said, 'I woke up this morning and I was still alive, so I am pretty cheerful.' That's the upside of growing old.

In Praise of the Full Sentence

It may seem arrogance on my part to disparage creative writing classes and it may be wrong to say they are always bad. I have attended some myself and have been fortunate in not hearing a stipulation of rules.

There are certain rules which journalists and those in business need to follow, of course. Here, the short sentence and short word are desirable. Newspapers like *The Mercury* are aimed at the reading level of a literate eight-year-old and of course the self must not intrude into a business letter.

Unfortunately, these rules seem to have entered the realm of literature. Use a full, even rather long sentence or a polysyllabic word, and the emerging work is struck down, as if a cardinal sin has been committed. Those who slavishly follow the rules are in danger of producing work suitable for a first grade primer, and the personal voice, which adds colour and interest to the piece, is eliminated.

Stephen Murray-Smith, in his valuable book *Right Words – a guide to English Usage in Australia* asserts, 'debasement of language leads to a debasement of feeling and thought', and I am in agreement.

I have moved somewhat from the praise of the fuller sentence to the use of fuller words. To deliberately choose on a regular basis the long and seldom used word is pretentious, but sometimes such a word is the very one needed. English is such a rich and nuanced language, having benefited from invasion, that the right word, if we are lucky enough or diligent enough to find it, is at our disposal and our writing will be all the better for it.

Sometimes, however, writers go to ridiculous lengths to avoid a common word and commit what has become a sin, namely to repeat the same word in a paragraph. I found an example of the former in a novel I was reading recently, when the gathering began to 'percolate' into the next room. If I had been the editor, I would have deleted that verb and been happier even if the over-used 'trickled' had appeared, but editors have different views on the use of language.

Short words, like short sentences, are popular these days, and not only with the young. Some are robust and used appropriately. What I am about to say here has an M classification, so please close your eyes if you fear defilement.

'Shit' is a robust word and the past tense is the slightly amusing 'shat'. Of course it is commonly used as a swear word but given its proper use – well, it has its place. A child is not taught to say, 'Mummy, I have defecated.' Families have their own words to describe the process, but why not return to Middle English and use 'shiten' or 'shat'?

Another robust word used with sickening frequency and mostly inappropriately is the F word which, squeamishly enough, my pencil refuses to write in full. As a description of the sexual act, it is well enough but the dictionary description is 'sexual *intercourse*' and that it is not. Intercourse involves communication between the individuals involved; an exchange of thoughts and feelings. The misuse of the F word is an example of the debasement of language.

The words of wise others always seem better than one's own so here is Dorothy Green (in Stephen Murray-Smith, *Right Words*, 'Who is Dorothy Green?'): 'You are told by experts that language has to change.' To which the only retort is that it does not necessarily change for the better and there is no reason it should change overnight because some illiterate ass has the microphone in front of his mouth.

Of course language changes. Words vanish, new ones appear, just as writing styles change, as ours seems to be doing, to suit the busy lives and butterfly minds of the day.

There is a place for reading matter with short, clever sentences – that which is such a boon for bedtime reading or at the airport or when one is tired – but even then we surely do not want to revert to something which reads like that first grade primer, do we?

There is something extremely satisfying about what T.S. Eliot describes as 'the intolerable wrestle / with words and meanings', and what I for one appreciate in my reading is when every phrase and sentence is right. (Where every word is at home / taking its place to support the others /the word neither diffident nor ostentatious / an easy commune of the old and new / the common word exact without vulgarity / the formal word precise but not pedantic / the complete consort dancing together.) It is a struggle but surely a worthwhile one.

If one thinks of the writing that has endured, the creators did not attend creative writing classes; they agonised over their work but spoke with their own unique voices. Think the Psalms of David, the stories of Dickens, the Brontes, Shakespeare, Jane Austen. Their sentences are not noted for their brevity. Nor are those of such contemporary writers as P.D. James, A.S. Byatt, Christopher Koch, David Malouf – the list is long. William Faulkner and Marcel Proust are noted for sentences which are not only full but flowing over. Faulkner has the honour of producing the longest sentence in the English language. In *Absolom Absolom* there is one comprising 1,288 words. Stream of consciousness novels such as James Joyce's *Ulysses* (which I intend to read one day) can be discounted.

It is plain that the long sentence and the little used but appropriate word do not mean that this authorial style equals obscurity. When we look at the literature that has survived, sometimes for centuries, we may conclude that the opposite is the case.

Look at Me! Look at ME!

I suspect we all know a few attention seekers. They do not exactly beat their chest and proclaim, like Muhammad Ali, 'I am the greatest', but they like to be seen as the life of the party and to dominate conversations; dialogue gives place to monologue. Get two attention seekers together and a dual monologue emerges.

These are the intentional attention seekers. Although their behaviour is often repellent, it is sometimes caused by an underlying lack of confidence or a sense of inferiority.

Flamboyant dressers, those with dreadlocks or multicoloured hair or with multiple tattoos or piercings, are often seen as inviting attention, yet they may be simply, in modern parlance, 'doing their own thing' or what makes them feel good.

I feel deeply sorry for the inadvertent attention seekers. I have good reason to empathise with them. I have to record that I blushed my way through my entire adolescence and beyond. That may sound rather sweet, like naivety itself, but a male teaching colleague pointed out to me that innocence is really ignorance and should not be considered a virtue. Some truth in that, but knowledge is often acquired through very painful experience. That takes time.

I taught and was resident at a boarding school for the deaf. There were male and female teachers. We took our meals in the staff dining room and sat wherever we chose or where there was a vacant chair. I dreaded the necessity of sharing the table with certain members of the male team because so many of the casual remarks I made were perceived as double entendres. I was often bewildered by their laughter and when comprehension dawned came the hated sensation of the rising blush.

When, on at least two occasions, I have walked briskly and confidently around town with my skirt rucked up behind (a curse upon swirly skirts) I certainly have not invited attention. I once pitter-pattered down Campbell Street from the site of the state school to the CBD in such a condition. It was only when a kind lady (bless you, my angel) tapped me on the shoulder and informed me of my state that I was able to remedy the situation and proceed with retrieved dignity.

In Salamanca Place, having emerged from what is now euphemistically called the 'bathroom', I was unaware of any attention my hinder parts were receiving until I heard a piercing whistle. It was not one of those two-toned whistles one once modestly ignored while secretly exulting but a whistle suggesting urgency. I turned to see a couple who mercifully happened to be my friends, with wild but explicit gestures indicating that (again) my skirt was rucked.

I hope these revelations do not suggest that I make a habit of appearing in partial undress.

There was an occasion on which I rather hoped I *would* gain some approving attention. It was in our interpretive dancing class conducted by a lady of European origin. We addressed her as 'Madame'. I rather fancied myself as one of Isadora Duncan's ilk as I floated around in my semi-transparent, wafting garb. At the end of the year display of Madame's group of dancers, I drifted around with the rest of them, gliding with undulating arms and pretty hand movements. I felt that Madame's eyes were fixed upon me quite intently and was elated by the thought that I was dancing particularly well.

At the end of the performance, Madame drew me aside, showing at least some sensitivity. 'Betty,' she said bluntly, 'you need a good uplift brassiere.'

My latest unintentional attention getter took place at a recent book launch. I swear it had nothing to do with the glass of red wine I was holding in my hand. I had taken but a sip. I was standing – perhaps not the most sensible thing for an octogenarian to do for any length of time – when I sensed that all was not well. Something unwanted and undesirable was about to happen. Sure enough, I began to collapse. I did not faint – THUMP – but folded up like a concertina, my wine spilling everywhere.

A kindest of kind friend standing by helped me onto the chair which some other solicitous person provided. I looked at the floor and was reminded of Duncan's blood – who would have thought the glass had so much (wine) in it? The floor was splashed, even some books spattered. The thoughts which pass through one's head on these occasions of semi-consciousness are strange.

A few years ago, I collapsed with septicaemia. On my stomach, because I was unable to crawl, I inched my way into my bedroom but could not climb onto my bed. I lay on the floor covered by the duvet which I managed to drag from it. Somehow, my head found its way to the underneath of my white-painted bedside table. All I could think was, 'Goodness! How dirty! I must wash it.' Never a thought that I was dying, which I was. My rescue is another story.

I wonder, when I *do* lie dying – beautifully, of course, hands on breast like an effigy in an ancient cathedral – will I gaze at the ceiling and think, 'Oh, my goodness! A cobweb'?

I digress, so back to those embarrassing moments. Had I ever cried, 'Look at me! Look at me!'? No. I am an unintentional attention seeker. Pity me.

My Room 101

Winston Smith's Room 101 was indeed horrible. The thought of being eaten by rats, beginning with earlobes and fingers, is shuddering stuff, guaranteed to bring about betrayal and compliance.

On a light note, my Room 101 would be filled with people all brainwashed into adding an intrusive neutral vowel into words like known, flown, sown, mown. Thus we have even ABC radio and television journalists and announcers saying things like 'If the prime minister had only knowen...', or maybe 'People who have flowen with Qantas...' and so on. What is the rationale behind this unnecessary intrusion? I don't know, but in such company I would confess to anything, betray anybody, if that would ensure my release. Well, perhaps not. Perhaps I would just descend into madness.

Seriously, my Room 101 would be filled with knives, all coming towards me like Winston's rats. 'Is this a dagger which I see before me / The handle towards my hand?' No. The daggers would be in other people's hands coming towards *me*.

If I hear the reportage of a murder where the killing has been done by a gunshot, I am deeply dismayed, of course, but if it has been done by stabbing I am appalled. It seems to imply vindictiveness beyond understanding and suggests lengthy and painful death.

I do not like my kitchen knives to be sharp, despite assurances that it is safer to use sharp knives rather than blunt ones. Less likely to cut oneself, it is said. A certain couple who stayed with me a year or so ago and were very helpful in the kitchen, sent me, soon after their return home, a set of knives. This thoughtfulness was touching but it was not a gift over which I rejoiced.

My nursing career was short, but even junior nurses were allowed to observe some surgical operations, with permission and in their own time. I opted to attend an appendectomy one day. The surgeon was handed his scalpel; he made the first incision and I was out of the theatre as fast as I could go. What had I been thinking of? Did I imagine that the patient's abdomen would respond to 'Open Sesame'? Not long after, there was an opportunity to witness a Caesarean section. I did not take it and today I rather wish that I had because one of my granddaughters has had two such procedures; but I would have had to observe that first laceration with the very, very sharp straight knife. Today I think the opening is made by laser.

I wonder whether politicians have a morbid fear of knives. They should have, because there is always the possibility of a stab in the back. '*Et tu, Brute!*'

Not Eden

'A garden is a lovesome thing / God wot', and indeed it is, but the struggle to create a beautiful 'rose plot / ferned grot' is not easily achieved, at least not by me.

There are times when, as I stroll around my block examining plants for black spot, aphids, thrips, mildew and all those other nasties that assail them, I do think that my garden looks quite pretty and occasionally even green and healthy. More often, as I pluck infected spotted or yellow leaves and chewed buds, I feel quite otherwise.

Deep despair sets in after I visit friends who own miniature botanical gardens. The leaves of their plants are green, glossy and unchewed; their flowers, almost always other than the reliable pelargoniums, agapanthus and hydrangeas, display their colourful exotic heads. The fruit trees are heavy with fruit and if there is lawn it is green and thick. I return to my own struggling Eden (and I expect that's an oxymoron) with a heavy heart and wonder what it is that is gnawing at the sad, long strappy leaves of the succulent which was supposed to be so resilient.

I am (to use a cliché) on the horns of a dilemma. Should I succumb to the current trend towards the replacement of grass with gravel; to the supplanting of roses and other flowers suited to English gardens with grasses and drought resistant anti-pest plants? I don't like those options.

In my back garden, I have a swing seat. I've always wanted one, for I have happy memories of serene moments swinging back and forth on one which graced the big veranda of a relative. I must have been six at the time so I've waited a long while before having one of my own.

Now, what I had envisaged was me, book in hand, swinging gently and occasionally looking up from my reading in order to relish the beauty of my 'rose plot / ferned grot', but no, such is not the case. When I do find time to sit thus, all I see are weeds to be pulled, discoloured pest-eaten leaves to be removed, the murky water in the bird bath to be replenished. The sight before me simply does not match the vision in my head. How much longer can I pretend that my untamed garden is really an Edna Walling one and this is the spot of wilderness that she recommended?

Once my husband gave me a book called *Garden Problems Solved* which contains photographs of diseased plants. The images are as horrifying as the illustrations in my medical book, the pages of which I ruffle through very rapidly as I search for the disease from which I feel I may be suffering. For every plant, there is a possible disease and the remedies seem to require more money and time than I am prepared to spend.

Friends give me cuttings and plants for which I'm very grateful but alas terrified that they might not thrive. Some do die, I'm sad to say, more from too much care than the opposite – too much water, for instance. When they do survive and flourish, I'm overjoyed and I associate each plant with the giver. I have four rose bushes given to me by a dear friend who has since died, so when they bloom I feel her presence. I was also given a flowering cherry when my husband died and the spring flowering evokes great joy.

When at times I reflect on a move to accommodation which has, say, a small courtyard, I imagine life without a garden and wonder, what then would nourish my soul.

'A garden is a lovesome thing / God wot.'

Red

I've always been interested in the fact that the name of a colour is so evocative. Most people, I believe, when thinking of white, will picture a bride or perhaps an angel; its antithesis, black, might create images of mourners or perhaps the chic black worn by women in Melbourne, Paris and New York – the cities, I'm reliably informed, which boast more of these wearers than any other.

My conscience and my purse will not allow me to buy glossy magazines like *Vogue* but there are places where they are accessible without charge: cafés, hairdressers, doctors' and dentists' waiting rooms.

Recently I was indulging in a coffee in a café which has piles of 'glossies' and I did choose an edition of *Vogue* which featured clothes which could only be termed 'wearable art'. No ordinary woman could possibly wear them. However, there was an article written about the year's film of *The Great Gatsby*. It was illustrated with photographs and the actor (apparently there are no actresses these days) who took the part of the unfortunate Myrtle was wearing the red dress. This was chosen because red, to quote the producer, is 'vulgar, brash and full of life', as indeed was Myrtle.

This rather alarming statement caused me some discomfort as I am a lover of red. Though I've never been brave enough to wear a completely red dress, I do like a crimson scarf, jacket or handbag. And I do like red shoes. I demur at being called vulgar or brash, liking to think that I am neither, but of course we do not see ourselves as others see us.

'Full of life' I would like to be and I think I was, once upon a time. In it was an element of impulsiveness, sometimes leading to mistaken judgements and concomitant punishments. No need to wait for hellfire, which, of course, is red.

Red is the colour usually associated with danger, yet to the Chinese it is the colour of happiness. My friend, married to a Taiwanese politician, once gave me a jade ornament on a red thread. It is a small facsimile of the armrest of an emperor's throne. It does not necessarily make me feel happy or powerful or lucky but it does remind me of a long and valued friendship.

Why is scarlet often seen as a harlot colour? There is a certain red known as carmine and so it seems fitting that the most famous of the operatic harlots is called Carmen. In the Handa operatic performance, the red dress worn by Rinat Shaham as Carmen was breathtaking; voluminous, swishing and difficult to handle.

The areas where prostitutes linger are known as red light districts. Yet was there not a place of dubious morality on the Hobart waterfront known as the Blue House, or is it a figment of my imagination?

Thinking now of blue, I wonder why Australian redheads were once called Bluey. There was a comic strip called 'Bluey and Curly', not in colour, I think, but it was made obvious that Bluey was a redhead. It's strange that redheads are not popular. Young people in particular describe the man of their dreams as 'tall, dark and handsome', never 'tall and redheaded'. On the other hand, women often have their hair dyed red. The shades differ and my eldest daughter, once a natural copper top, now greying, chooses to use henna and is sometimes a rather eye-catching sight. When we meet, I take a deep breath, zip my lips and soon get over it. My son was a redhead too, his hair almost honey-coloured, and thick. What self-respecting McKenzie would sport anything else?

When walking the streets of Edinburgh many years ago, I was struck by the beauty of the many red-headed girls I saw. I have a very vivid recollection of one who had flawless skin and startling green eyes. Redheads in Australia are not served well by the climate. Not only do they have ravaged complexions but they are unfortunate candidates for skin cancer. They also have to remember the biblical warning, 'Look not thou upon the wine when it is red / when it sparkleth in the cup / for it biteth like the serpent and stingeth like the adder' for the Celtic complexion becomes unbecomingly flushed with too much sipping from the cup.

I don't think I've ever received that symbol of love, the red rose, though I have been given flowers. A dozen red roses – or even one – left on my doorstep today would cause me to wonder rather than send my pulse racing, but it would be nice.

Scarlet roses were my husband's favourite flower and when he was bedridden I planted a bush outside the window facing the bed. I was so glad that it grew quickly so that in the summer in which he died I was able to gather a bunch of blooms to place in a vase where he could see them.

Red. One could write a book about it. There's been no mention of rubies or beetroot, of blood or lipstick or red sky in the morning. A disciplined writer would forget about dishes, dusting and unmade beds; would sit quietly and wait for further evocations arising from the mantra-red.

The Fix

Ferdinand Cortez may not qualify for sainthood since he is chiefly known for the destruction of a whole civilisation. But he did one good thing and that was to introduce cocoa in the sixteenth century. A 'cocoa house' was opened in London in 1657 and the burgeoning cocoa houses became 'centres for the fashionable and the wits'.

Is there a person in the world who does not enjoy chocolate? I certainly have never met one. Where chocolate is concerned, I myself am not a gourmet but a gourmand; to put it bluntly, a glutton.

You have to be very old, as I am, to remember the little wafer-like threepenny bar of Nestlé's chocolate. There were not too many spare threepences around but when one came my way, I knew exactly how to spend it at the local general store. For the same sum, one could buy a paper bag filled with broken biscuits but the chocolate bar was vastly preferable.

A box of chocolates, maybe Black Magic, used to be part of the courting ritual, along with the gardenia or the orchid corsage. The latter seems to have vanished. Indeed, where could it be pinned? Where a dress had been, there is now flesh. The former has remained and why? Chocolate is addictive. Fortunately, this addiction has been pronounced good. This is not necessarily good for gourmands because the good chocolate is the dark bitter kind, not the pseudo, creamy, fatty ultra-sweet one. A large Cadbury's milk chocolate is a no-no for those whose diets preclude it or for those who aspire to a neat waistline.

As a young mother determined to have my children grow up with strong healthy teeth entirely free from decay, I did not give them sweets except on Fridays, when our evening meal comprised a mixed grill followed by a chocolate frog for each child instead of the usual dessert. It was not surprising that this was the favourite meal of the week.

When, as a family, we had a three-month sojourn in Harrogate, Yorkshire, a special treat was to have afternoon tea in the wonderful cream cake and chocolate shop called, perhaps appropriately, 'Betty's'. There we also bought a box of chocolates to take to the Christmas pantomime. The box was covered in faux red velvet and the whole event – the snow outside, the cosy theatre and the marvellous chocolates – seemed to have been extracted from a story in one of the Christmas annuals so popular at the time.

The Domain Writers, of which I am a member, are fortunate indeed to meet in Salamanca Place, where the chocoholics' heaven is sited. Norman and Dann have chocolate of every kind: milk, white, dark, filled, embellished. Those decorated with exquisite flowers would win the chocolate equivalent of the Nobel Prize.

Hitherto unknown to my fellow writers, I sometimes sneak into N and D on my way to Franklin Square, where I board my homeward bus. I buy one chocolate-covered fig. 'The biggest,' I direct, 'and don't wrap it.' I nibble it as I walk along.

However, my favourite chocolate is the one with the chilli 'fix'. The Mexicans are to thank for that too. They made a frothy drink with cocoa mixed with spices, one being chilli, so good for mental health. The endorphins are released, and happiness, if only temporary, ensues.

And there is good news, my friends. Endorphins are supposed to regulate pain and hunger so there is much to recommend the Chocolate Diet. Can it be so easy to be happy and slim? I feel some verses coming on. Please, poets, please cover your ears.

> My aspirations don't stretch far
> Can't write a book like *Chocolat*
> However, there's no other sweet
> Which constitutes a greater treat.
>
> The very name has resonance
> Accompaniment to high romance.
> A velvet box with heart like shape
> Adorned with bows of satin tape
> Causes maidens' hearts to flutter
> And miffed wives to melt like butter.

And ovoid shapes at Easter time
With rabbit cards and sugary rhyme,
Hollow or filled with caramel
Are always sure to go down well.
Endorphin-filled, the cocoa bean
Praise be! will ensure that we are lean.

Terrorists on the Café Strip

We all know about terrorist groups and their heart-stopping deeds of cruelty. Most feel fear when they hear the names: Al Qaeda, the Taliban, and ISIS. Perhaps you may not be aware that there is another terrorist group in our midst. It has infiltrated the major cities of Australia and sneaked into trendy outposts like Noosa or Daylesford. There are probably cells in places back of Bourke.

I'm referring to the rise of the Baristas. They make no effort to conceal themselves. They have no need to. Men and women both are drawn to them, needing their service to get through the day or to recover from the night before.

Perhaps you are scoffing at the very notion of the Baristas being a terrorist group but while the word terrorism can be an ambivalent one, depending which side you are on (the alternative title being freedom fighter), there can be no doubt that the relevant term is the first.

Consider what a terrorist is: one who favours the use of intimidation and more often than not uses violence. As far as I know, the Baristas have not resorted to murder but their attitude is often akin to torture.

Ask for a coffee in a café and the Barista enquires coldly (because of course you should *know* what kind of coffee you want) whether you are ordering *café au lait, café noir* (and should it be short or long) a cappuccino, a caffè latte, a mochaccino, an affogato – the list goes on. More varieties are no doubt being invented even as I write. I might add, though, that a Dutch coffee, which was, in days of yore, simply a cup of black coffee with milk, seems not to have a place on the list. Too simple for words.

Well, having selected your coffee, opting for the safest – say a long black or the ubiquitous cappuccino – because you are not sure what the others are, you sit and wait for the beverage to arrive. You wait…and you wait…and you wait. Is there perhaps some delay in the shipment from Brazil?

Time was, and I certainly remember it, when you entered a café, asked for a coffee with or without milk and very shortly a cheerful waitress would bring it to you. Now the brew has to be made by a disciplined person with a certificate who is in charge of a sinister metallic machine with multiple handles, the manipulation of which results in explosion, hisses and steam. If any innocent thinks to snatch a quick cup of coffee before work or between appointments or wants to grab one while briefly catching up with a friend, that naif should forget it. Already intimidated by the scornful gaze of the Barista who has realised that your ignorance of the permutations of the caffeine brew is abysmal, it takes a really courageous or desperate person to confront the terrorist, asking why it is taking so long to produce the drink.

I recently took this brave step and as an excuse for his tardiness he said, 'Look,' and with a sweep of his arm encompassed three other customers, 'I'm really, really busy. I have to deal with *all these*!' Defeated by his fierce look, I slunk to my seat. Cowed, I humbly waited. When my coffee arrived, the far too deep froth was decorated with a swirl that was certainly not a heart.

I speak as an almost Sydney girl (since I lived in that city from the age of twelve until twenty-one) when I mourn the days, long gone, when a sixpenny cup of coffee at Repins was delivered in a couple of ticks, as was the new and exciting cappuccino of the 1940s, the drink of ultra sophistication served in the dear little Marguerita in trendy Rowe Street.

The Barista, armed with an intimidating supercilious look and a gleaming machine which, I suspect, can at any moment be turned into a weapon of mass destruction, is an unavoidable terrorist to be defeated by the memorisation of innumerable types of coffee potions and the ability to kill with a look.

The Lowbrow: a response to her critics, with the help of Alexander McCall Smith

All right, all right! I know you think I should be wrestling with *Ulysses* instead of enjoying Alexander McCall Smith but listen, the latter writes lucidly; he amuses while challenging the reader to think about moral issues. His style is almost deceptively simple but he is never afraid to see that, in the words of T.S. Eliot (just to show that I *can* extend myself in the way you may think desirable) '...every word is at home / Taking its place to support the others.' Be it long or short, 'The common word exact without vulgarity / The formal word precise but not pedantic.'

He seeks the right word, long or short, not *deliberately* short, simply to be kind to the reader – how patronising is that dictum. What an adventure it is to meet a new word and to have to look it up – perhaps in an actual book with pages – and so fully understand the context. Another jewel is added to one's lexical necklace.

McCall Smith helps preserve our wonderful, beautiful, nuanced English language even if his works are not deemed literature in the sense of works of 'superior or lasting artistic merit' (*Australian Oxford Dictionary*).

Reading his books, my lost words re-emerge. They have been lurking in shadowy areas of my brain since they are not in common use – not by me at any rate. 'Suzerainty, shibboleth, quotidian' – I encounter new ones. I did not know that 'immanent' meant 'inherent' – I can hear the moan of highbrows. What a 'perjink house' is, no dictionary of mine will tell me. I think it must be some strange Scottish adjective.

Married to a doctor, McCall Smith always expands one's medical knowledge. I am now familiar with what afflicted one resident of 44 Scotland Street, poor Mitty Antonia. In the Uffizi gallery, she beheld the original *Birth of Venus* and succumbed to Stendhal's syndrome. I thought that the author had mischievously invented this phenomenon but no! It is actually a form of hysterical reaction that affects some people when they come face to face with great art. Now, would anyone have learnt that from reading Marcel Proust? I have not read anything of Proust's but his work is dubbed 'Literature'. All I know is that he spent a great deal of his life in a bed with dirty sheets and that he was given to profound thoughts while dipping a madeleine in his cup of tea. If that is all that is needed to induce profound thoughts, I must try it. I guess a digestive biscuit would do as well.

Smith is funny and cheeky. In a recent publication, he reintroduces his fans to the dwellers of 44 Scotland Street. He mentions that one of them, the artist Angus, was drinking coffee in a café when, through the glass window, he espied a black-clad, fashionably stubbled man whom he eventually recognised as Ian Rankin. Ian gave him the thumbs up and walked on. He is actually a friend and neighbour of Smith's and this was really an irrelevant, cheeky interspersion. However, it reminded me that I am a fan of Ian Rankin's too. A friend and neighbour of mine dismisses crime novels as thumb-suckers. I do not care. His prose is fashionably economical; there is conversation on every page, natural and often pithy. I am sure he could be a literary writer if he so desired. Listen to this:

> It was one of those cool crepuscular days that could have belonged to any one of at least three Scottish seasons; a sky like slate roofing and a wind that Rebus's father would have called snell.'

I looked up 'snell' in my bible, the *Macquarie Dictionary*, and found the word is a noun and is 'a short piece of gut or the like, by which a fish hook is attached to a longer line'. That is rather mystifying, so the Scots must use it as an adjective meaning I know not what. Googlers may be able to save the mystery. Please let me know.

On the subject of obscurity, perhaps some may share my bewilderment upon reading some examples of contemporary poetry. It seems that there are new rules: no rhyme, no metre and certainly no punctuation. It must be contrived and obscure so dunderheads are left far behind. Pity those poor lowbrows who agree with John Keats when he wrote to John Taylor in 1818, 'If poetry comes not naturally as the leaves to the tree, it had better not come at all.'

Of course there is wonderful free verse that meets that criterion, but is anyone moved, improved or delighted by verse such as this?

> false lick feint soft! Fast! winking vinegar florid ever
> dream clocks in at butter; ensign pariah physical slush
> swine mutters, time out for tears.

This is an excerpt from a poem by one Bruce Andrews, of whom I know nothing and life is too short to be bothered to investigate.

The reading life of this lowbrow is quite wonderful. A book of witty comic verse is often my companion at bedtime. Strangely, it is not always easily understood because the poets are, almost without exception, very erudite, but I go to sleep with a smile on my lips.

I can read thumb-suckers without shame and I sometimes go very happily to bed with Alexander.

The Men in my Life

The title of this piece suggests that I will run through a list of steamy romances. I am sorry to disappoint you.

I have no inclination to write about the silliness of adolescence or the mistakes made by a young naive adult. Before the grand passion of my late forties, steamy romances were vicarious ones, on the whole, with men like Walter Pidgeon, James Stewart, Gregory Peck (especially Gregory Peck), Henry Fonda and gentlemen of that ilk. Today's chisel-jawed romantic hero does not appeal to me at all. There are no fevered liaisons between me and the men who are currently in my life.

My next-door neighbour is a bachelor with whom I have a conversation as he commences his morning walk with Dougie, his little dog. We speak in the front garden as I sweep up the daily visiting cards my resident possum leaves for me under the birch tree. This neighbour once saved my life, but that is another story. Needless to say, I am forever in his debt.

I am always pleased to see my gardener who is also a friend. He *does* greet me with a chaste kiss on the cheek. I enjoy his company when work pauses for elevenses. We have interests in common and like to exchange news of our families. He rather likes to slash and burn so I have to keep his lopping tendencies under control. I beg him not to prune without my consent but he cannot curb himself and does so all the same.

My bus men friends (I use the word loosely) seem to be disappearing. One, I know, has died and I sadly watched his physical deterioration. The Exercise Man whose conversation is always interesting has not been seen for some time. I hope there has been no catastrophe. He has fled from one of those strange countries which are featured in black tales like those of Dracula-like characters.

A very down-at-heel man who is often on my bus spoke to me as I sat next to him while waiting at the stop at Sandy Bay. I did not particularly want to as I could smell his whisky breath, but I was toting heavy bags and needed to rest.

'Hello, fellow traveller,' he said. His voice was pleasant.

I concentrated on our continued conversation, consciously suspending judgement about his mottled complexion, bulbous red nose, straggly hair and grubby clothes. I constantly tell myself not to judge people by their appearance because I have so often been proved to be wrong. Sure enough, our dialogue was easy and I discovered that he had been at university with a certain Tasmanian politician. I thought it a doubtful privilege, but still…

Our bus arrived and we did not sit together. He alighted further on in Sandy Bay and I wondered, as I watched him walk down a street leading to the waterfront, whether he was the black sheep of some prosperous and so-called respectable family. So easy to weave stories.

I am sorry to disappoint you. That is almost the sum of the men in my life, family excepted. Hardly material for a Mills and Boon.

'To Be or Not to Be'

It was all very well for young Hamlet to go about cogitating 'To be or not to be.' He had, if he so chose, his whole life ahead of him and, what is more, he could have spent it with the beautiful Ophelia if he had not been so beastly to her. He had no need to act as God and mete out punishment.

No, it is not the 'to be' that troubles me these days; it is the 'not to be'. It is a sin now, of course, to be elderly but our leader would certainly dismiss the easy solutions to this blight. Imagine these people who have turned seventy, retired from work and apparently no longer of use to society. What is more, they may need some financial aid from the dwindling number of taxpayers. They could be lined up and dispatched by gunfire in no time at all – *budget balanced!* A more humane solution would be to legislate for voluntary euthanasia, sadly off the agenda with the present government.

At times, I cannot help feeling guilty about being elderly and alive. I am acutely aware that I am part of 'the problem of the ageing'. At the same time, I observe my peers and do not understand why they should be thought of as a problem. They still engage with life and contribute to society, supporting their families emotionally and, very often, financially. They mind grandchildren, great-grandchildren; try to make the world a better place by being peace activists or environmentalists. They are politically aware and sometimes, legs allowing, join protest marches when they believe that their politicians are doing the wrong thing. Are these people problematic? Octogenarians and nonagenarians they may be but, to use the vernacular, 'still going strong'.

Inevitably, the senses fail and the brain cannot cope with complexities or even, unfortunately, with simple problems. At the same time, the eroded body is continually in pain and individuals often long to close the door on life. 'To be or not to be' is a question asked perhaps more often than we imagine. It takes courage to decide not to be and there is no help on hand. No longer do families care for their aged and when the latter are placed or persuaded to move to a nursing home there are often sad stories of their being forgotten.

A long time ago I stayed for six months in the parental home of my best friend. A treasured member of the family was her ninety-year-old grandmother, a tiny, self-effacing quiet woman and a devout Roman Catholic. I carry an image of her in my mind. I was walking past her bedroom when I saw her kneeling by her bedside, praying. She was in a white cotton nightdress and her still thick hair was braided and hung down her back. I'm sure she had no need to wonder whether to be or not to be.

What's in a Name?

'What's in a name?' asked Juliet of Romeo. Well, a lot, I can tell you.

I've never been much enamoured of my own first name – Betty. Well, it's my only name and seems suitable for a cow or, to elevate it, a domestic of some kind. I am not denigrating domestic work. I am thinking of the 'Yes, ma'am' servants in Victorian novels. I know a dog called Betty.

I am the younger of two sisters. My sister, the first born, was christened Joan Winifred; Joan was a common name in the 20s. Somehow it holds more gravitas than Betty. One thinks of the noble if misguided Joan of Arc, a saint no less. Winifred has never returned to favour but Joan was granted the appellation because our mother's maiden name was Winifred Miller Page. Besides bearing the name I do, insult is added to injury because I cannot boast a second name. Just how unimaginative can parents be?

My maternal grandmother, who died in the dreadful influenza pandemic of 1919 and thus I never met, was Elizabeth Fernie and that I like very much. Why could I not have been christened Elizabeth in her honour? That name has been favoured by queens and princesses, by dames and other notables. Think Queen Elizabeth I, Elizabeth Empress of Russia, Queen Elizabeth II and her mother the Lady Elizabeth Angela Marguerite Bowes-Lyons; poet Elizabeth Bishop, writers Elizabeth Gaskell and Elizabeth Taylor and the actress of the same name, never forgetting the biblical Elizabeth who miraculously gave birth to John the Baptist.

To return to Joan: we know about Saint Joan but who has ever heard of a Saint Betty? I do not think I have the qualifications to be the first. Come to think of it, I believe Queen Elizabeth II was known to the family by the diminutive but once she was crowned, was she ever called Queen Betty? Of course not!

There are names which are stored in my memory – nice exotic

ones. Not one of them replicates mine. Beulah Elaine Claudine Snook was a school friend, and a beautiful girl in a senior class was, somewhat unbelievably, Dusk Hannah. A very tall classmate with memorably large feet was Petal Gough. I will wager that her parents were rather dismayed when their flowerlike babe grew to proportions more resembling a tree. The granddaughter of one of my friends has been christened Antigone, which does not seem such a wonderful choice considering the Oedipus story, but it is certainly impressive. Her diminutive is the rather charming 'Tiggy'.

I do not long to be a Clarissa, Olivia, Vanessa – one of those females who marry Sebastians, Hugos and Christophers who shop at Harrods and have high tea at the Savoy – but I *would* like to be an Elizabeth with a nice second name like Jane or Ella or Lucy, a name that shows evidence of deep parental thought.

Instead, I have been awarded what must be the ultimate insult. The front page of a recent edition of the *Mercury* features a photograph of a man holding a Tasmanian devil, now the official animal emblem of the state. The caption reads, 'Bonorong Wildlife Sanctuary head keeper, Jason Graham, with *Betty the Tasmanian devil*' (italics mine).

I have a good mind to break out and commit some devilish deed bringing my name some notoriety but all I can do is mourn and moan, reflecting on the words of one Marshall McLuhan, 'The name of a woman is a numbing blow from which she never recovers' (*Understanding Media*).

Gone but not Forgotten – a Eulogy

In the 70s, three of my closest, dearest friends died. They were in their fifties, had lived rich lives and anticipated fulfilling years ahead. Their children were young adults and almost independent. They were free to develop their own interests, fortunate in having husbands who certainly were developing theirs so did not create impediments.

I could write about any one of them at length and feel sure that each life would be of interest to a reader but I have made a choice and her name was Julie Kershaw. Her husband is dead and her children are scattered throughout England. There is no need for pseudonyms.

Julie was convent-educated and a member of a strict Roman Catholic family in which she felt unloved. She married very young with a strong desire to create a warm, loving family. Such an early commitment proved to be a mistake.

She entered my life when she came to Chambersbury Junior School in Hemel Hempstead, where I was teaching. She was what we would call a teacher's aide, hoping to eventually train as a teacher. Although her husband had a very well paid job with the BBC, there were then six children to be fed, clothed, housed and educated. Education was one of the top priorities. All the children took music lessons and two of them, in adulthood, had musical careers, one as a violinist in an orchestra, the other as a composer of background music for television programmes.

Life throws up miracles and Julie was one of them. She was a fine seamstress, as convent girls of that era seemed to be. She made clothes for the children and for herself and always looked as if she had stepped from the pages of *Vogue*. In an interview for an article in the local newspaper, she told the journalist that she was not a methodical person but this was certainly not true. She ran a very tight ship.

The children had their set duties – as did her good-natured, lovable, lazy husband. Their bed sheets were changed on different days so that their mother did not have seven sheets to hang on the line. Top sheets were transferred to the bottom so that there would not be fourteen to be washed and dried. No room for seven on the line let alone double that number. These days, she would have had a clothes drier. Perhaps she did, later.

Shoes were cleaned, clothes were hung up and household chores shared. The youngsters set off for school each day with pressed clothes, shining hair and pocket handkerchiefs. Sammy the youngest, though only three, was admitted to kindergarten and went to Chambersbury School with his mother.

Julie saved my family – my then husband, our three children and me – from spending our first Christmas in England rather lonely and homesick. She invited us to share Christmas tea with them and it proved to be a delightful evening. The house, of course, was immaculate, tactfully decorated, and the Christmas tree a pleasure to behold. We were to share more Christmas evenings with the Kershaw family in the years to come.

I am not quite sure whether Julie thought that our Australian children should be gentled but on one occasion she took our granddaughters, Hannah and Jemima, to afternoon tea at the Savoy. I am sorry to say that the girls were singularly unimpressed, though I am sure they gave polite thank-yous.

From time to time, Julie would tell me that she was weary (as indeed she had every right to be) and was going to a retreat. She would be away for a few days, with her husband holding the fort. It was not until much later that she confessed that she had spent those days with her lover, a doctor trapped in a very unhappy marriage, as was she. I met him and indeed they seemed to fit together like two pieces of a jigsaw puzzle. He was handsome and charming and shared her interests, music in particular.

Apart from running her household so smoothly, she was secretary of the Mayor's Cancer Appeal Fund and of the local hospital League of Friends.

The good doctor planned to divorce his wife and marry Julie, who had already divorced her husband. She was no scarlet woman and had tried for a long time to make her marriage work. Some might agree with Shakespeare (Sonnet CXVI) that there should be no impediment to the marriage of true minds.

Sadly the doctor, faced with an hysterical wife, changed his mind and returned to his unhappy marriage. Julie's ex-husband wanted her to remarry him and, mistakenly, she did. Of course, neither of them had changed. They were still incompatible. There was no hate but no joy.

Julie found herself a career as a medical representative and, unsurprisingly, gained an award as the highest achieving medical rep in Hertfordshire. I am not sure what she thought about the drugs she persuaded the medics to try or whether she believed the blurb that went with them.

Julie's eldest daughter, who had a special place in her parents' hearts, died from a rare blood disease. She was in her twenties and newly-wed. When she was first ailing, Julie helped raise money for research into the condition by walking across the Grand Canyon in Arizona.

After the young woman's death, something died in her mother. There was a grief which nothing could eradicate.

My last meeting with this dear friend was in 1984 when I flew to England to visit my eldest daughter, who had married an Englishman. She and I spent a happy day in London and I remember trotting beside her, pitter-pattering in order to keep up with the strides only long legs can achieve. We were crossing the road to reach Liberty's, my favourite store, when a Rolls Royce almost bowled us over, stopping with a jerk to avoid doing so. It was the driver's fault, not ours. Julie banged on the bonnet and raised an admonitory hand. She was like an imperious queen. Somehow that image remains in my memory.

It was on this visit that I noticed that she had a persistent dry cough and there was an unusual fragility in her appearance. She dismissed the cough as unimportant.

I returned home and we continued to correspond. Her letters were always a pleasure to read. She kept an eye on my daughter and always treated my grandchildren with great kindness. It was fortunate that they lived in a nearby village.

When Julie was fifty-nine, she rang me to give me the news that she had advanced lung cancer. She laughed when she told me that she looked in the mirror and saw a yellow face. I am not good at the stiff upper lip and could not help shedding tears. She detected this and told me not to be sad but I *was* sad and continue to be.

I remember her as a good friend and a remarkable woman; gone but not forgotten.

'There's a Divinity that Shapes our Ends'

A friend of mine often makes purchases which she later regrets and I'm sometimes the beneficiary of her mistakes.

The latest error, resulting in my most recent acquisition, was the buying of an abdominal control garment which came with the promise of flat stomach and Cuban buttocks. There were accompanying directions for actually getting into it – no easy matter since, unfilled, it was about the size of a pot mitt, with legs.

Trim'n Lift was the name of this creation and the instructions for putting it in place were as follows:

> Hold waistband and roll down to crotch gusset, insert your legs and slowly roll waistband to your hips, insert your hand and lift buttock to required position, adjust 'Trim'n Lift' to your waist.

I stopped at direction number two. If I *had* succeeded in inserting my buttocks into the pouches provided, I would *not* have had high, tight Cuban buttocks but would have become a suitable partner for a Hottentot since Hottentots choose their wives by the size of their derrières, preferring these to be ample – or so I've heard.

Now, all this brings me to the subject of control garments in general since, on reflection, they have featured quite largely in my life and probably in the lives of my female contemporaries. These days, our bottoms are allowed to be free floating, as it were, a situation not tolerated in the centuries leading up to this one.

At thirteen or so, I looked forward quite eagerly to the day when I would travel into Sydney with my aunt and be fitted with a corselette by her corsetière. The corselette was a light garment made from some material with little perforations in it and was a combination of bra and belt with suspenders appended – two in front, I think, and two behind. It was lightly boned, and slumping would result in a jab beneath the bosom. To be imprisoned in a corselette was a kind of rite of passage on the way to female adulthood.

My aunt was measured for an altogether much more rigid garment. This was the corset, featuring bones, hooks and laces all working together to make it fearsomely tight.

My poor sister, older than I, was considered a candidate for this initiation into full womanhood and when she finally wore her very own corset to church she was the subject of much mirth from her peers because the silence of prayer was punctuated by the creaks which accompanied every breath she drew.

I had my own encounter with a noisy corset when, as a young teenager, I travelled from Sydney to Melbourne to stay with my married cousin, the daughter of my previously mentioned Bathukolpian aunt. In those days, the journey on the Spirit of Progress was an overnight one and, as I travelled second class, this involved sitting up all night. The lady sitting next to me, one of ample proportions, took pity on me (quite unnecessarily, as it happened) and invited me to rest my head on her knees. This was expected to promote sleep. I was a shy child and didn't like to refuse the offer, so dutifully did as she suggested. The sleeplessness! The agony! Every time the woman breathed, her corset creaked and, to make matters worse, my cheek and ear rested (perhaps not the appropriate word) on her knobbly suspenders. What a relief to reach my destination!

I was spared the confinement of the corset by the fortuitous arrival of the roll-on, also known as the step-in. This was an elastic foundation garment without fastenings, relatively easy to put on and offering a degree of comfort unknown to the corset wearer. Like other supporting garments, it was hot in summer, but women were meant to suffer, weren't they?

The suspender belt came next and was rather a sexy article, often trimmed with lace, and, because it bore the ubiquitous suspenders, as the name suggests, it was the partner of silk or, later, nylon stockings. It gave considerable freedom but sometimes had a tendency to move sideways, or was that because I chose the wrong size?

All praise and honour to the inventor of the next supportive garment – the panty girdle! No suspenders and worn, if desired, with the other marvellous innovation, pantyhose. Or it could be worn without, by which I mean not *outside* but *sans* hose.

Ladies of mature age probably stick with the panty girdle and find it as difficult as I would do to come to terms with the non-supportive G-string or the aptly named thong. I have seen these articles on a clothesline and they resemble wet curling rags (remember them?) and appear to be inimical to comfort.

What next, I wonder? Simply that 'brave vibration each way free' as Herrick (?) would have it. Not for me. I'm off to study once again the directions for the use of the Trim'n Lift – there *must* be a way…

Surviving without Fractions and Dots

I have to be honest: I am a bear of very little brain. It amazes me that I have friends with great intellectual capacity and I am even more astonished that they seem to enjoy my company. I sometimes wonder whether I act as a kind of foil so that their cerebral light shines brighter in comparison with mine – a mean thought, which somehow persists. It was once reinforced when someone enquired of me, 'How is it that you have such intelligent friends?' Surely that was a prize-winning back-hander, from which I am still recovering.

At high school, our English teacher, Mrs Ross, also taught us mathematics – tried to teach the latter, in my case. There were probably a few others of almost equal ineptitude but when I confess that she sometimes asked, after some mathematical exercise, 'Did anyone else *besides Betty McKenzie* get that wrong?' you will understand the gravity of my disability.

As an adult, I can add, subtract, divide and can certainly give the change from five dollars which, I believe, is the test for numeracy. However, fractions and decimals can cause confusion. Let it be known that I am in exalted company because Lord Randolph Churchill himself famously confessed, 'I never could make out what those damned dots meant.'

It was Zeus who gave Pandora that famous box that she was not supposed to open. The forbidden is always attractive to the young so, of course, open it she did. Out flew a multiple (goodness! I've used a mathematical term) of evils. Poor dismayed Pandora – but *Then* out flew Hope. The world was comforted.

Well, my box was pretty much like Pandora's but out flew a good fairy called Graphomania, the urge to write. That served me well, for I used to come top in Mrs Ross's English class and so was partially redeemed.

Mrs Ross did once disturb my peace of mind outside academia. (Can one call high school academia?) There was a family holiday spent at the hotel, Caves House, at Jenolan Caves in New South Wales, an unusually posh holiday. As we were entering the dining room on the first evening, who should be almost in step with us but Mrs Ross. Her beady brown eyes fixed upon me. I was grateful that apparently she had not brought a supply of chalk with her, otherwise a piece would have been shot in my direction, as it was wont to do in the classroom, accompanied by a fierce stamping of the foot as she cried, 'Nonsense! Rubbish!' when offered an erroneous solution to a problem. She cast a shadow, albeit faint, over the whole holiday.

When that nice jovial economics man on ABC2 informs us about the status of world currencies, I ignore the worth of the British pound and the Australian dollar, although I receive payments in both. Forget the numbers, I think, just remember that if one goes up the other goes down so I have an idea, just sufficiently clear, of what I will receive.

My condition – and there is a name for it, a bit like dyslexia, only concerned with numbers – was not helped by my dear late husband, an engineer and a very able mathematician. It was not unusual for me to be awakened on a cold wintry morning by a question such as 'If we were to invest x amount at x per cent how much would we gain if…?' That is about all I grasped and I chose to consider the question rhetorical. It was effort enough to achieve even a foggy consciousness.

He liked to tease and test. I remember him asking, while I was busy dealing with the manageable numbers a recipe required, 'What is the cube of two?'

'Eight,' I replied crisply and was amazed that the answer had been stored in my brain, to be retrieved at exactly the right moment. 'Gotcha!' I thought.

A man with a great sense of humour, he related a mathematical joke just minutes before he died. It was very funny. It is hard to believe that I have forgotten it.

My inability to grapple with mathematics except at the very lowest level has not greatly affected my life, though every now and then it causes me embarrassment. Forgive me if what follows sounds self-laudatory. My aim is to convince you that I am a survivor.

I have managed to word my way through three university degrees, words alone saving me from failure in one case. Wrestling with statistics, in part because I was unable to attend all the lectures, I wrote a letter to Dr M suggesting that I withdraw from his course in special education since statistics were irrelevant to classroom activities and that if I were presented with raw data, I would give it to a statistician to interpret. To my surprise, this explanation was accepted. I was reprieved; my studies continued. Is this degree fraudulent?

To write a definitive essay on the subject of survival of an almost innumerate – or indeed on any subject – is in my case an achievable goal but I take comfort from Montaigne, that lovely man, who offers consolation to anyone struggling with fractions and damned dots, or any other flaw. He counsels them to learn to live with imperfections and even to embrace them. So I do, and I hope I have made my point – yet another mathematical term!

Luxury

Bending over the washbasin while cleaning my teeth seems a funny place to suddenly begin to think about luxury, but that is what happened one recent morning.

Perhaps it was because my bathroom is the place of simple pleasures which some people – in developing countries, for instance – would consider great luxuries. The morning sun shines through my bathroom window and caresses my skin when I emerge from what I certainly consider a luxury – the daily hot shower. Cleansed and warmed, I can face the day.

What exactly is luxury? Is it that which is beyond necessity? If so, we can dispense with cars, TV sets, smart phones, all forms of computers, washing machines, refrigerators. I am being random in my selection. We *could* do without these things but they have somehow morphed into necessities for most people.

I did a tiny piece of research, asking some of my peers what they considered luxury. Only one gave the immediate response, 'A five-star hotel.' I was a little surprised because I would never have thought her materialistic, but I came to understand her response when she added, 'I could be alone for a while without noisy dogs and a noisy husband.' I know that she is happily married. She explained that her husband is a big man and rather clumsy. I imagine him as lumbering.

Other responses without exception focused on warmth: a hot shower, an electrically heated bed, a warm foot bath, a warm climate. Quiet was also mentioned. There was no reference to expensive cars, large houses containing pneumatic sofas and chairs, indoor lap pools, golden bathroom fittings and similar excesses featured in glossy magazines.

It is easy to denigrate luxury related to excess, but without some excess, surely we would be living in caves. Paintings are not essential, nor are sculptures, flower gardens, wonderfully designed houses or clothes. So artists of every kind are unnecessary as are horticulturists, architects, the list goes on. Simplicity has its place but how dreary life would be without the luxuries I have mentioned, and of course there are many more. There are millions of people who do not have these things, do not have the basics like shelter and food, and how worse than dreary their lives are.

My own luxuries are coming home after a full day, sitting in my warm room, seated on my rather hard old settee, spooning hot soup into my more than willing mouth; waking in the morning knowing that I do not have to leap out of bed but can lie in the warmth (that word again) and listen to the news before coffee and the delight of hot porridge.

Amongst many there is a desire to return to a life of simplicity, to live close to nature. To these people, simplicity is now a luxury and difficult to attain.

I recall the words of the Persian poet Omar Khayyam, who expressed beautifully the ultimate luxury. 'A jug of wine, a loaf of bread and thou.'

The Evocation of Colour

Last week, I had afternoon tea in the home of a friend. It is a residence such as one sees in glossy magazines like *Belle*.

For as long as I have known her, she has favoured earth colours; not so much the vivid orange of desert sand or the pinks and purples of Uluru at dawn and dusk but dun colours like mole or squirrel. Can these latter really be called colours?

Now the monochromatic look is definitely 'in' but my friend's taste for it has remained constant for the fifty or so years that I have known her. Her rooms are those you would expect to have photographed for publication. Not only do the dun colours blend but the furniture is perfection; crafted, not mass produced. Everywhere there are *objets d'art*, carefully arranged, each piece of latest design. There are no garage or op. shop sale items like those which cause members of the *Collectors* team to become feverish with excitement. Photographs are not on display and the only painting hanging on the wall – if painting it can be called – is a framed bold signature of some contemporary artist.

I admit that the atmosphere created is restful but I wonder if I could live happily in such a setting. I really do crave colour as well as 'a sweet disorder', to quote Herrick. I have to admit to a passion for red. Give me a room with neutral colours and I almost immediately see a place for it.

In my bedroom, I have white bedside tables and on my bed is a white cover. My curtains (spare me the word drapes) are purple *toile*. The pelmet is covered with the same but I felt the need for crimson piping and when that was done I felt deeply satisfied.

On the mantel in my lounge room I have a red ceramic clock – a serendipitous find – and my favourite painting, given to me by the artist, Ali Leereveld, is of a woman dressed in scarlet.

To my great delight, friends who were recently my house guests presented me with the most exquisite glass rooster. It has a crimson comb and claws. Its feathers are red, green and blue.

I don't know why I favour a colour often associated with harlotry or, at the least, coquetry. I don't like to think that there is some deep vein of untrammelled lust buried somewhere in my being. I expect I should be glad, however, that I have no vampire tendencies, as I can't stand the sight of anyone else's blood. This could explain the brevity of my nursing career.

Can the love of the bloody hue be indicative of something other than those already mentioned?

I can't help thinking of the poetry of Sylvia Plath. She was obsessed with red but in her case it is associated more with death than passion, so often she refers to blood. Even when she describes mud ('Getting there'), it is 'thick, red and slippery'; her wellingtons ('Letter in November') squelch through the 'beautiful red'. She refers to herself as 'red meat' and in her poem 'Tulips' those flowers are seen as loathsome.

The Evocations of Colour

The tulips are too red in the first place,
they hurt me.
Even through the gift paper I could
hear them breathe
lightly, through their white swaddling,
like an awful baby.
Their redness talks to my wound, it,
corresponds.
They are subtle: they seem to float, they
weigh me down
upsetting me with their sudden
fingers and their colour,
a dozen red lead sinkers round my neck.

Our favourite colours say something about ourselves. To Plath, red is death but I prefer to associate it with passion – not lust but zest for life.

Lexical Gold

New words were once stored in my memory but these days are more likely to find their way to my forgetery and that has begun to overflow. The egress, I fear, may be lost forever but that doesn't stop my lexical acquisitiveness.

The other evening, I tackled a crossword puzzle, as is my wont, and for the first time in my life encountered (eventually and through the good office of a friend) the word 'smoot'. It was the answer to a scientific clue and not to be found either in my thesaurus or my science and technology dictionary. I am a Luddite and do not use a computer so haven't the help of Dr Google. However, my friend does have a computer and was able to consult the *Maverns Word of the Day* page. She discovered the answer to the cryptic clue. It was 'smoot'.

Now there's a lovely word which simply lends itself to doggerel, but I must resist. It seems that 'smoot' was first recorded in the seventeenth century and is of Scandinavian origin. It has several meanings and I'll relate them because you'll surely want to choose and use one of them one day, even at the risk of total incomprehension from listener or reader.

Choose one of these: a narrow passage, a covered alley, a hole or opening at the bottom of a fence, a stone used to block that hole. Or use it as a verb: in printer's slang, a freelance at a printing house where one is not usually employed; or to creep under or through. Thus one could 'smoot' through a 'smoot', I suppose.

The meanings which I think have the most utility are 'the absolute variant of smut' or the Middle English past tense of 'smite', thus 'I smut him'.

The absolutely marvellous use of the word is as a unit of measurement – initially for the length of the Harvard Bridge which links the

Massachusetts Institute of Technology with Boston and which is 364.4 smoots and one ear long.

I quote:

> The Smoot is named after Oliver Reed Smoot, junior. Mr Smoot was a pledge at the Lambola *chi alpha*: when the pledges were ordered in 1958 to measure the length of the bridge, they used Mr Smoot, who was the shortest in that particular class, as a ruler. He was just five feet and seven inches tall.

I didn't promise that I wouldn't rhyme. I can't help it!

Lexical Gold

As a family we're not tall,
We could, in fact, be labelled small
And, alas, as well as that,
We have a leaning towards fat.
So happily my grandson measured
(A solid fact that will be treasured)
Much more than Daddy in his teens
Because he eats his meat and greens.
At thirteen (and he thinks this beaut)
He is exactly *one whole smoot*.

Legs – a female view

Lately, the subject of legs has been very much on my mind. Like every bodily part, the extremities are taken for granted when we are young. They're just there and if we're fortunate, as most of us are in the salad days, they function perfectly well, so we don't think about them very much.

However, apart from their utility, there are some physical features which are apparently important in the mating game. I'll skip reference to the upper part of the body and more downwards to the legs.

Julia Blake's husband, whose name eludes me, said in a past radio interview that he fell in love with Julia's legs first and then moved upwards to her face, which happens to be a particularly beautiful one. This seems strange to me but there's no accounting for the workings of the male mind.

It is plain that the long leg with the slim thigh and the slender ankle, for males the desirable one. I've never read the Kama Sutra and know of it only by repute, so can only suppose that there is some connection, and certainly the long leg would be more suited to dangling from the equivalent of the chandelier than the short one.

Apart from the aesthetics, it is the convenience of the long leg which is the cause of my present annoyance or rather, my lack of it. As a traveller on a bus which has to negotiate many sharp curves on the Channel Highway as it moves towards town, I have to cling to the armrest of my seat to avoid falling to the floor and rolling around like a dried pea. Some drivers seem to think that they are competitors in a grand prix. If I'm sitting facing the seat in front of the wheel well, my legs are simply not long enough to brace myself by placing my feet on its casing. It is supposed to serve the purpose of stabilising the passenger when necessary but there has been no thought given to the owners of peasant legs; short and sturdy legs made for walking and working.

Should such a person be fortunate enough to be offered a lift in a car, you would think she would feel undiluted gratitude, but there's a catch. I've often watched, usually on TV, tall, long-legged women slide gracefully into car seats. They obey the dicta: first place your bottom on the seat then swivel elegantly and draw your legs (together of course) into the car. Mission beautifully accomplished.

In many cars, this is not possible for the owners of peasant legs. The bottom is plonked down as instructed but do the legs follow? No. With much grunting, the right leg makes its way to the floor but the left remains unbecomingly stuck out. As Robert Graves wrote in his poem, Legs, 'Resolutely nowhere / In both directions.' With luck, there's that little hand grip above the car door which one can hang onto while tugging the left leg in. I mean 'tugging' – it's such a help to be wearing trousers; they can be clutched at the knee and act as a hoist. Wearing a skirt is not the best thing, for that can result in an unseemly display of knees, not always a pretty sight.

I'm actually not scarred by being the owner of the aforementioned legs. They have served, and still are serving me, very well and did not dash my marital prospects, but I do still wish that I could slide into a car with a model's sinuous grace.

Bogans

The term 'bogan', as far as I know, has not reached the *Macquarie Dictionary*. Mine is an old edition, and it may well be in the latest. However, most people have their own idea about what constitutes a bogan. Some picture this entity as one who wears trousers with the crotch around the knees, a hooded jacket or a cap worn backwards, both distinctly grubby. They hear the voice – rough and sprinkled with expletives. They note the ignorance of grammar and the lack of any elaborated sentences. They are sure that they come from the northern suburbs, the equivalent of Sydney's 'westies'. They are considered louts, bores, hoons, illiterates.

The other day, I was in town and thought I'd undertake a mini-research. I had some shopping to do so I asked each of the young people who served me how they would recognise a bogan. These were the responses: 'badly dressed and dirty', '[rough] speech', 'pyjamas and uggies in the mall'. More kindly, 'someone a bit rough about the edges' and 'someone who lives past the Flannel Curtain'. I didn't know where the Flannel Curtain was so, on enquiry, was told that it was beyond Creek Road, New Town.

When I dropped in to the Flight Centre to have a word with my travel agent, I asked for her definition of bogans and she replied, 'Rough nuts in the mall'. A young man at the nearby desk called out, 'Tasmanians!', a response which elicited cries of outrage. 'Sorry, sorry,' he said quickly. 'Only joking.' He confessed to coming from New South Wales.

The rest of the day was spent with my sixteen-year-old granddaughter, Ella, so over lunch I continued my research.

Ella informed me that bogans have tribal tattoos, wear baggy jeans, like to hang out in the mall, speak harshly and ungrammatically, and 'just don't know how to behave'. She added, 'They've never been taught.'

Apparently, bogan girls, who seem to be less visible, comb their hair back but leave 'bogan bits', very thin dangling strands of hair on either side of the face. They often favour flared trousers.

It was a happy coincidence that the next day on Radio National, Callum Scott, an academic and an authority on boganality, gave a talk on that very subject, adding yet another definition of a bogan (not his own) as one 'who has long hair at the back, short at the front and [is] pissed all day'. Scott himself added two more characteristics – being racist and sexist – but suggested that these were overt attitudes in bogan culture but were held covertly by many of the middle class. He dared to cite Howard and Abbott as nationalists of the worst kind.

On a lighter note, he pointed out that leisure wear is a uniform worn by all classes of people but the middle class participate in sport and the others simply watch and this did conjure up the TV image of Norm slouched in his chair with a tinnie in his hand.

As a bus traveller, mostly on the Taroona run but sometimes on one heading for Moonah, I am able to observe many young people and as far as dress is concerned, there is often little to distinguish a bogan from any other young people. They are uniformly rather grubby and crumpled and their footwear nothing other than soiled runners.

So how to distinguish one from the other? Listen to the voices. I've heard showers of expletives from both but some pronounce them ever so *naicely* so of course they're not bogans.

And what of loutish behaviour? Only yesterday as I travelled home on the bus, I sat next to a youth with piercings (not exclusive to the culture on which we're focusing), tattoos and a mullet haircut. The bus was crowded and a woman of mature years was forced to strap hang between the two inward-facing seats. Opposite me was a well dressed man in his thirties. Which of the two offered the woman his seat? The one whose appearance might have branded him a bogan.

It is easy to judge and label people by externals and I think we all do it but shouldn't. Brutish behaviour, too, is found in all sections of society but is less obvious in those who have the twin shields of money and education. Demonising bogans, without knowing them as individuals, is surely boorish in the extreme.

Uncle

Whenever I propose a subject, it boomerangs and renders me partially insensible so that I then have to struggle to meet my own challenge, but meet it I will, for better or for worse.

It's a sad fact that we often fully appreciate friends and relations after they have departed this life. We think back on their actions, some of which we positively resented when we were young and they a force in our lives.

For many years, my sister and I were in the care of an aunt and uncle, two kind and generous people who decided to have us join them and our two cousins and become part of their family.

It is this particular uncle I'm thinking about, as I often do these days. I can only now see that he was in many ways a remarkable man. He was of short stature but conducted himself with such dignity that we hardly noticed his lack of height. An industrial chemist, he worked in the laboratory at the Mortlake gas works, outside of Sydney. He went to work suited and always wearing a most unfashionable butterfly collar, a collection of which had to be sent out to be laundered each week. At weekends, he would don casual trousers and a short-sleeved shirt and had the unfortunate habit of wearing, as many English men still do, socks, with what my children irreverently call 'Jesus sandals'.

He was not an effusive man and the only kisses I observed were the chaste ones he planted on my aunt's cheek when he arrived home from work. However, he treated children with respect, never talking down to them and always taking an interest in their schoolwork and hobbies.

Mealtimes were sometimes a bit of a trial because, absorbed as he was by philosophy, he often indulged in long, philosophical monologues. Dialogue was impossible as none of us – and that includes my aunt – then understood what he was talking about. The philosopher most mentioned was Bertrand Russell. Uncle was a Fabian socialist and a great admirer of George Bernard Shaw. He emulated Shaw in his eating habits and my long-suffering aunt cooked him a vegetarian dish for dinner every night while we tucked in to aromatic roasts and casseroles and luscious desserts. Uncle ate sparingly and I don't remember his eating sweets at all.

The end of dinner ritual was the making of coffee which Uncle undertook with a chemist's precision. Water was boiled in a small saucepan then the coffee grounds and a pinch of salt were added. It was left to stand for three minutes precisely before it was strained and served in demitasse cups which Uncle's potter sister made. We took for granted those little cups with the butterfly handles. Coffee was accompanied by a pre-cut cube of cheddar. Moderation in all things.

The other day, I searched in vain for Uncle's last letter to me. His handwriting was as exquisite as it was idiosyncratic and I haven't the words to describe it. Absolutely symmetrical and somehow delicate, it was deserving of a frame.

He once penned his favourite poem for me and I know that it embodied much of his personal philosophy.

> Turn, turn my wheel,
> The human race
> Of very tongue and every place,
> Caucasian, Coptic or Malay,
> All that inhabit this great earth
> Whatever be their rank or wroth
> Are kindred and allied by birth
> And made of the same clay.
>
> Longfellow, 'Keramis'

Although his father was a Methodist minister and, I imagine, coming for the pottery town of Burslem in Staffordshire, one of the fiery kind, Uncle was not a Christian in the traditional sense. He believed in a presiding powerful spirit and would have respected the beliefs of any of the great religions as long as they taught respect or love for their fellow human beings.

In my spare bedroom, I have a little antique secretaire which was given to me on my sixteenth birthday. It was a present from both my aunt and uncle but chosen by the latter. It has secret drawers, with cards on which are printed the months, the days and the dates, so that they can be changed daily. There's a little white slate (if it can be called such, because it isn't slate) upon which notes can be written. I think of Uncle when I see it and remember other acts of kindness: how his fascination with astronomy led him to set up his telescope on the back lawn so that we could see and name the constellations, names which I regret to say I have forgotten; how he mended our school shoes and varnished our school cases; how he demonstrated his socialism by undertaking the care of two virtually orphaned girls alongside his own son and daughter and bought a house for a relative who had been hard hit by the 30s depression.

His last letter stated that he had a slight stomach problem when in fact he knew he was dying from stomach cancer.

All these virtues I now recognise, and understand the words which Shakespeare put into the mouth of Antony: 'the evil that men do lives after them; the good is oft interred with their bones'.

The Winner Is…

This is not the first time I've written about undergarments. I'm beginning to worry that my friends will think I have an unhealthy obsession with lingerie. This is not so, although difficulties do arise when one wishes to buy just the right brassiere. One wishes that engineers who know so much about bridges, cranes and the like and, in particular, scientists who study the forces of gravity, would undertake to contribute this knowledge to perfect that article.

The other day as I sat in my local and favourite café, where sitting and reading for some time while drinking coffee is not frowned upon, I happened to pick up a copy of the latest *Kingborough News*. The Kingboroughians in my area are on the whole quite sober people, many committed to saving the world and growing their own vegetables, so I was somewhat surprised to light upon a small item of news entitled 'Innovative lingerie'. Not a thought on this subject had been on my mind but of course I was intrigued.

Not long before, I had listened to a talk on Radio National – Robin Williams's science programme, I think – in which I learnt that there is an award for scientific research which has scant hope of being very useful. I'm sure the award is fictitious and purely titular. It is known as the Ignobel Prize. Three examples were given. One scientist has apparently discovered how to *un*boil an egg. I suppose this proves that cooking is chemistry; hence a domestic science school is not a misnomer. Another researcher has found that any mammal over three kilograms in weight takes exactly twenty-one seconds to urinate. This excepts humans. It is hard to imagine how that piece of intelligence can have practical application. One other contender for the prize weighed the tail feathers of a chook, surmising that its resultant walk would be like that of a dinosaur. Interesting.

It seems that 'a Japanese lingerie firm claims to have developed a bra that pops open when a woman is in love'. It is unclear whether the bra opens at the back or at the front; probably the latter, as the alternative would hardly be noticeable let alone spectacular. The Japanese bra apparently monitors the wearer's heart rate and 'sends the data via Bluetooth to a mobile phone app'. (The latter part of this explanation might just as well be written in Bulgarian for all the sense it makes to me, Queen of the Luddites with a virgin iPad on the study desk.) Only when it is satisfied that the wearer is in love will the bra unclasp. Further, this is supposed to protect women from unwanted advances. How? Will the woman protest, 'No, no, no! I'm not in love with you?' Such a response would surely not be sufficient protection.

And there's another hitch, as the small article rightly pointed out. There are other situations in which the heart rate might increase: at a job interview, for instance. The possibility of employment could be greatly diminished – or, on reflection, perhaps not.

Another thing. The wearer of this wonder bra might be truly in love but the object of this adoration might not be reciprocal. Embarrassment all round, I think.

So – the winner of the Ignobel Prize is…

www.ingramcontent.com/pod-product-compliance
Lightning Source LLC
Chambersburg PA
CBHW030915080526
44589CB00010B/320